SPORTS
ALL-ST★RS

SAQUON BARKLEY

Jon M. Fishman

Lerner Publications ◆ Minneapolis

Lerner Publications Company
An imprint of Lerner Publishing Group, Inc.
241 First Avenue North
Minneapolis, MN 55401 USA

For reading levels and more information, look up this title at www.lernerbooks.com.

Main body text set in Albany Std 15/22. Typeface provided by Agfa.

Library of Congress Cataloging-in-Publication Data

Names: Fishman, Jon M., author.
Title: Saquon Barkley / Jon M. Fishman.
Description: Minneapolis : Lerner Publications, [2020] | Series: Sports All-Stars | Audience: Ages: 7–11. | Audience: Grades: 4 to 6. | Includes webography. | Includes bibliographical references and index.
Identifiers: LCCN 2019013427 (print) | LCCN 2019019578 (ebook) | ISBN 9781541583597 (eb pdf) | ISBN 9781541577268 (library binding : alk. paper) |
Subjects: LCSH: Barkley, Saquon, 1997—-Juvenile literature. | Football players—United States—Biography—Juvenile literature. | Running backs (Football)—United States—Biography—Juvenile literature.
Classification: LCC GV939.B375 (ebook) | LCC GV939.B375 F57 2019 (print) | DDC 796.332092 [B]—dc23

LC record available at https://lccn.loc.gov/2019013427

Manufactured in the United States of America
1-46748-47739-9/6/2019

CONTENTS

Running Up the Score. 4

Facts at a Glance. 5

Football Plans 8

Big Lifter. 13

Making Statements 18

"A New Style". 24

All-Star Stats 28

Source Notes 29

Glossary 30

Further Information 31

Index 32

RUNNING UP
THE SCORE

Barkley rushes against Washington in 2018.

The New York Giants had a 10-point lead against the Washington Redskins on December 9, 2018. Running back Saquon Barkley was about to make New York's lead even larger.

- **Date of Birth:** February 9, 1997

- **Position:** running back

- **League:** National Football League (NFL)

- **Professional Highlights:** chosen with the second overall pick in the 2018 NFL draft; finished second in the NFL in rushing yards in 2018; won the 2018 **Rookie** of the Year award

- **Personal Highlights:** holds many weight-lifting records at Penn State University; saves most of the money he earns playing football; bought his parents a new house

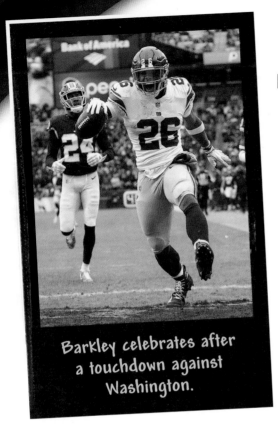
Barkley celebrates after a touchdown against Washington.

Barkley took the ball behind the **line of scrimmage**. He shuffled his feet as he decided which way to go. Then he cut to his left and raced past the Washington defense. He was so fast that no defender could touch him.

Barkley cruised down the field. He ran toward the corner of the **end zone** and jumped with joy as he scored. The 78-yard touchdown run made the score 17–0. But the Giants weren't done scoring yet.

Later in the game, Barkley rushed for 52 yards to help the Giants score again. They had an enormous 34–0 lead in the third quarter. That's when Barkley showed he's almost as good at catching passes as he is at running.

It was third down. New York needed to gain three yards for a first down. Quarterback Eli Manning stepped back. He saw Barkley to his left and threw the ball. But a defender ran to break up the pass. Barkley reached beyond the defender and grabbed the ball with one hand. The incredible catch gave New York a first down.

The Giants got another touchdown, making the score 40–0. Most of the second half was still to come. But with such a huge lead, New York's coaches pulled Barkley and some others from the game. The backup players got a chance to play. New York won the game 40–16.

Barkley racked up 170 rushing yards despite sitting on the bench for most of the second half. It was his highest rushing total of the season. Barkley was a rookie, but he was already a key part of the team. "We're starting to figure out that . . . this offense runs through him," Manning said.

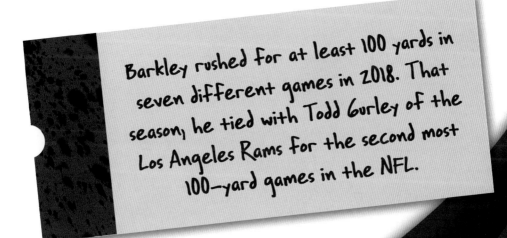

Barkley rushed for at least 100 yards in seven different games in 2018. That season, he tied with Todd Gurley of the Los Angeles Rams for the second most 100-yard games in the NFL.

FOOTBALL
PLANS

Barkley rushes for Penn State in 2017.

Saquon Barkley was born in the Bronx on February 9, 1997. The Bronx is a **borough** of New York City. Saquon's father, Alibay Barkley, had been a boxer. But Saquon's sport was football.

Barkley attends the 2018 NFL draft with his parents, Tonya and Alibay.

When he was three years old, he told his father that he would grow up to become an NFL running back. He also promised his mother, Tonya Johnson, that he would buy the family a house one day.

Saquon's family lived in a dangerous neighborhood. His father had been involved with drugs and crime as a teenager. After Saquon was born, his father began using drugs again.

Barkley loves sports. While visiting a high school football team in 2018, he even tried coaching.

His mother had relatives in Pennsylvania. On family visits, she noticed that Saquon and his siblings loved the fresh air and freedom to run in the grass. She remembers thinking, "This is where I want to be. My children look happy here." Hoping to give her family a better life, she decided they would move to Coplay, Pennsylvania.

The new start did wonders for Saquon's father. He quit using drugs and got more involved in his children's lives. That included taking Saquon to a lot of football games and practices.

Saquon played football at Whitehall High School. As a sophomore, he began to play games for the **varsity** team. But he spent most of his time on the bench. In one game, the starting running back was injured. Saquon replaced him. Coach Brian Gilbert remembers Saquon's first play of the game. "It was right up the middle for about 52 yards for a touchdown," Gilbert said. "I remember all the coaches saying, 'Maybe we should be playing him more.'"

Barkley ran track in high school. In the NFL, his speed helps him outrun other players.

Barkley played three seasons with the
Penn State Nittany Lions.

Saquon started playing more and impressing everyone who saw him. He even drew the attention of college **scouts**. His success made him work even harder. He lifted weights and ate healthful food. He boxed, played basketball, and competed in track and field. "I love [track and field], but I'm doing it to keep in shape for football," he said.

The hard work paid off. Barkley graduated from Whitehall in 2015. His next stop was the Penn State University football team.

Barkley shows off his skills at the 2018 NFL Combine, where college players work to impress scouts.

Barkley began spending hours in the Penn State weight room each week.

A scoreboard hanging in the weight room keeps track of the all-time Penn State football team records for eight different lifts and **drills**. Barkley holds the running back records for all eight.

Barkley's leg strength powers his incredible leaps during games.

Barkley lifts massive weights to build his strength. One of his favorite moves is the **power clean**. He lifts a **barbell** from the floor to his chest while standing. Barkley set the all-time power clean record for a Penn State football player in 2017. Two weeks later, he broke his own record with a power clean of 405 pounds (184 kg)!

Barkley practices with the Nittany Lions in 2016.

Barkley kept lifting weights in the NFL. He says strong legs help him pull off powerful moves during games. When defenders grab him, he can use his legs to break free and keep running. "I want to be known as a guy who breaks tackles," he said. "That's the whole objective of the game."

Barkley doesn't eat much before games. Too much food upsets his stomach. He might have a light meal, such as chicken and potatoes.

In the NFL, Barkley started to focus on exercises that make him more **agile**. He steps through a grid on the ground in one drill, moving his feet as quickly as possible.

He likes to work out barefoot on the sand. It takes extra effort to run on soft, shifting sand. Barkley might run with an elastic band around his ankles or a **parachute** attached to his back. The special gear makes his workouts even tougher.

Barkley does drills to stay light and fast on his feet.

Barkley attends the NFL draft in 2018.

At a barbershop in Pennsylvania in April 2018, just days before the NFL draft, Barkley made a major fashion statement. He wore a hooded sweatshirt with the New York Giants logo on the front. The sweatshirt sparked excitement among football fans. The Giants held the second overall pick in the draft.

Barkley poses with NFL commissioner
Roger Gooddell during the draft.

Did the sweatshirt mean Barkley knew the Giants were
going to pick him?

Rumors swirled over the next few weeks. Some said
New York was definitely going to take Barkley. Others
thought the Giants wanted to trade away their pick. The
draft finally arrived on April 26. New York chose Barkley.

Though Barkley prefers to save, he likes to shop for designer shoes.

Barkley wasn't used to people noticing his fashion choices. He doesn't usually buy fancy clothes or expensive cars. Instead, he saves most of his money. And he has a lot to save. The Giants pay Barkley millions of dollars each year. When he joined the team, they gave him a bonus of more than $20 million.

Barkley also earns money by partnering with brands such as Pepsi and Nike to help sell their products. Barkley uses this money for his living expenses. He wants to save the money he earns from football for the future.

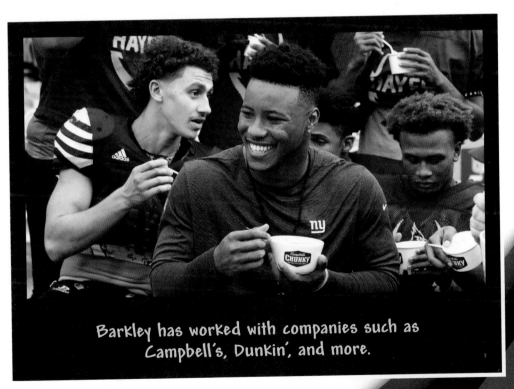

Barkley has worked with companies such as Campbell's, Dunkin', and more.

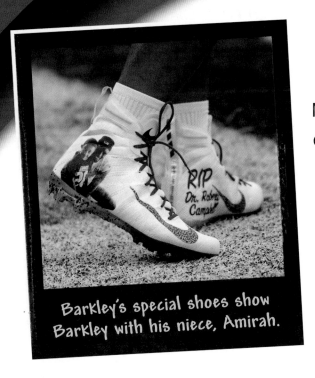

Barkley's special shoes show Barkley with his niece, Amirah.

Soon after joining the NFL, Barkley made one large purchase. He bought his parents a new house in Pennsylvania near where he grew up. His mother picked the house and the location. Barkley had fulfilled the promise he made to her when he was three years old.

Barkley uses his money to help others too. In 2018, he announced that he would wear special shoes during games. The red-and-white shoes showed Barkley with his niece, Amirah, who has a disease called 22q. The shoes made people more aware of the disease. Barkley also donates money to support more research into 22q.

Machiavelli Barkley

When Saquon was born, his father wanted his son to have a special name. His father loved hip-hop music and suggested naming the boy Tupac Shakur in honor of the famous rapper. He also liked Machiavelli in honor of Shakur, whose nickname was Makaveli. Saquon's mother rejected those ideas.

They agreed on the name Saquon partly because it was different from other people's names. Saquon's mom liked the way Saquon Barkley sounded. And it was similar to Shaquona, Saquon's older sister's name. Since childhood, Saquon has had the nickname Say-Say.

Barkley and his parents attend a ceremony honoring him on March 24, 2018, a date his hometown declared Saquon Barkley Day.

"A NEW STYLE"

Barkley sprints for the end zone in 2018.

It's hard to predict who will succeed in the NFL. Even top draft choices can fail and leave the league quickly. But Barkley proved in his rookie season that he has the skills to stick around for a long time.

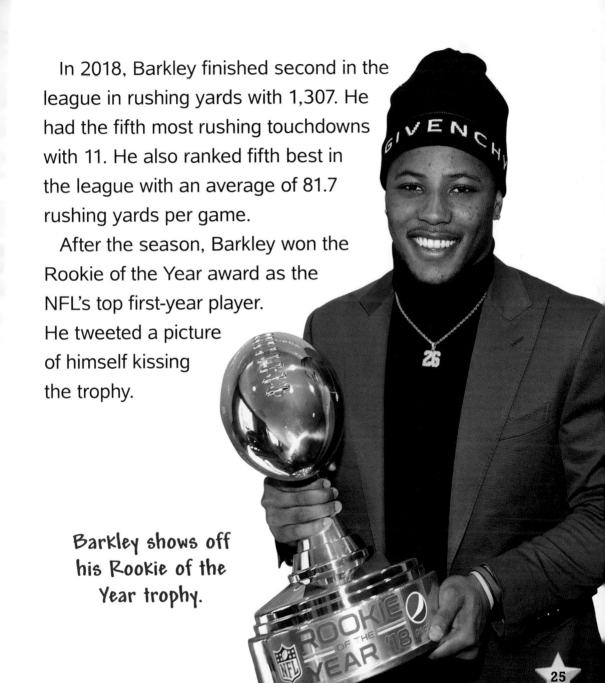

In 2018, Barkley finished second in the league in rushing yards with 1,307. He had the fifth most rushing touchdowns with 11. He also ranked fifth best in the league with an average of 81.7 rushing yards per game.

After the season, Barkley won the Rookie of the Year award as the NFL's top first-year player. He tweeted a picture of himself kissing the trophy.

Barkley shows off his Rookie of the Year trophy.

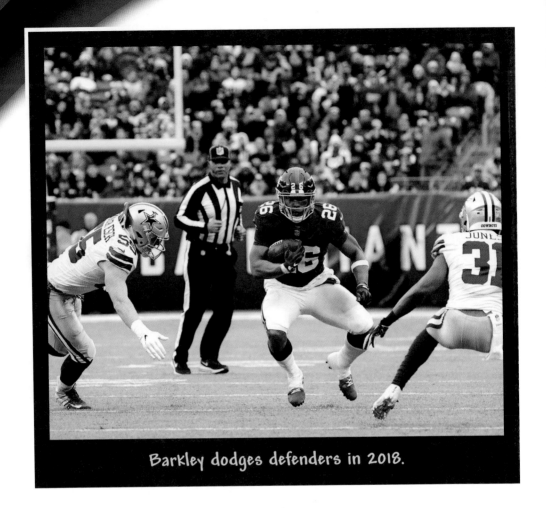
Barkley dodges defenders in 2018.

Sports fans love to compare athletes to one another. When a new star arrives in the NFL, fans begin wondering whom the player could be like. Will he have a long and legendary career like some of the all-time greats? Barkley isn't interested in being like anyone else. "I want to be compared to Saquon," he said. "I want to be my own guy . . . I want to bring a new style of running back to the NFL."

Barkley hopes to lead the Giants to the Super Bowl.

AROUND THE LEAGUE

All-Star Stats

Good running backs gain a large number of rushing yards during the NFL season. Good wide receivers rack up receiving yards. But some of the greatest players can do both. Here's where Barkley ranked in total yards gained for the 2018 NFL season:

Most Combined Rushing and Receiving Yards in 2018

Player	Position	Total Yards Gained
Saquon Barkley	running back	2,028
Ezekiel Elliott	running back	2,001
Christian McCaffrey	running back	1,965
Todd Gurley	running back	1,831
Julio Jones	wide receiver	1,689
Tyreek Hill	wide receiver	1,630
Alvin Kamara	running back	1,592
DeAndre Hopkins	wide receiver	1,565
Mike Evans	wide receiver	1,524

Source Notes

7 Associated Press, "Barkley Rushes for 170 Yards, Giants Rout Redskins 40–16," *ESPN*, December 9, 2018, http://www.espn.com/nfl/recap?gameId=401030753.

10 Jourdan Rodrigue, "Saquon Barkley and the Power of Choice," *State College (PA) Centre Daily Times*, September 2, 2016, https://www.centredaily.com/sports/college/penn-state-university/psu-football/article99490147.html.

11 Dan Labbe, "Who Is Saquon Barkley? His High School Basketball Career Will Give You an Idea," *Cleveland.com*, April 16, 2018, https://www.cleveland.com/browns/2018/04/saquon_barkley.html.

12 Michael Blouse, "Selfless Act by Whitehall Sprinter Saquon Barkley Had Some in Tears," *Allentown (PA) Morning Call*, May 13, 2015, https://www.mcall.com/sports/varsity/mc-district11-track-championships-barkley-panek-20150511-story.html.

15 Hallie Grossman, "Saquon Barkley Spills on Those Viral Lift Sessions," *ESPN*, June 24, 2018, http://www.espn.com/nfl/story/_/id/23853857/new-york-giants-rb-saquon-barkley-hurdling-lifting-record-breaking-body-issue-2018.

26 Steve Serby, "Saquon Barkley Will Put in Work for This Explosive Giants Offense," *New York Post*, July 21, 2018, https://nypost.com/2018/07/21/saquon-barkley-will-put-in-work-for-this-explosive-giants-offense/.

Glossary

agile: able to move easily and quickly

barbell: a metal bar with adjustable weighted discs attached to the ends

borough: one of the five divisions of New York City

drills: exercises designed to improve a skill

end zone: the area at each end of a football field where players score touchdowns

line of scrimmage: an imaginary line that marks the position of the football at the start of each play

parachute: a large piece of fabric used to slow the movement of something through air

power clean: an exercise with a weight that is raised from the floor to the chest and then dropped

rookie: a first-year player

scouts: people who judge the skills of athletes

varsity: the top team at a school

Further Information

Football: National Football League
http://www.ducksters.com/sports/national_football_league.php

Mack, Larry. *The New York Giants Story*. Minneapolis: Bellwether Media, 2017.

Monson, James. *Behind the Scenes Football*. Minneapolis: Lerner Publications, 2020.

New York Giants
https://www.giants.com

Savage, Jeff. *Football Super Stats*. Minneapolis: Lerner Publications, 2018.

Index

Barkley, Alibay, 8–10, 23

Coplay, PA, 10

Johnson, Tonya, 9–10, 22–23

Manning, Eli, 6–7

New York Giants, 4, 6–7, 18–19, 21, 27

Penn State, 5, 12–13, 15

Rookie of the Year award, 25

running back, 4–5, 9, 11, 13, 26

rushing yards, 7, 25

touchdowns, 6–7, 11, 25

weights, 12–13, 15

Photo Acknowledgments

Image credits: Patrick Smith/Getty Images, pp. 4, 6; Christian Petersen/Getty Images, p. 8; AP Photo/Ben Liebenberg, p. 9; Rob Kim/Getty Images, pp. 10, 21; Joe Robbins/Getty Images, pp. 11, 13; Ned Dishman/Getty Images, p. 12; Jennifer Stewart/Getty Images, p. 14; Abby Drey/Centre Daily Times/Getty Images, p. 15; AP Photo/Julio Cortez, p. 17; Rich Graessle/Icon Sportswire/Getty Images, p. 18; Tom Pennington/Getty Images, p. 19; Matt Winkelmeyer/Getty Images, p. 20; AP Photo/Bill Kostroun, p. 22; AP Photo/Joe Hermitt, p. 23; Grant Halverson/Getty Images, p. 24; Theo Wargo/Getty Images, p. 25; Steven Ryan/Getty Images, p. 26; Sarah Stier/Getty Images, p. 27.

Cover: Elsa/Getty Images.